ASH'S TO ASHES

Love, Suicide, Break up, Forgiveness

Carson Ellis

BookLeaf Publishing

India | USA | UK

Presentation by *BookLeaf* Publishing

Web : www.bookleafpub.com

E-mail : info@bookleafpub.com

ISBN : 9789358361506

First edition 2021

This book is dedicated to my "Mafata" and my "Mamata", you have always been there by my side pushing me to follow my dreams, pushing me to write this book. Well, guess what? It's finally here.

ACKNOWLEDGEMENT

I want to thank a very special person in my life, Hayden Bay, who restarted my love for writing. Without you, this book would never have happened.

Secondly, I would like to thank Christa Romaldi, my former boss, for teaching me about deadlines, and always being a light in my life. When things get bad you can always make me smile. Without you I would not have had this book ready by the deadline.

Miss Sarah Burke for introducing me to slam poetry through bringing Holly Painter into our school for a workshop. From that day I haven't stopped writing, and Holly Painter will always be one of my all-time favourite poets and inspirations. If it weren't for Miss Burke, I would have never found my love for poetry.

Jeremy Bider, I would like to thank you for allowing me to using your gorgeous photograph as my book cover.

Mrs. Dana Wright. My grade 10 history teacher, thank you for believing in me, and supporting me through high school. I would not be here today without your support.

Tracy Brownlee, you have never actually been my teacher, but you taught me so much more through experience than anyone could ever teach me in the classroom. You taught me that I have strength. A lot of inner strength, and I need to use it to make a positive change. Thank you for pushing me to do my best, and always cheering for me on from the side-lines.

Will Perre, my scuba diving instructor. Thank you so much for believing in me and finding ways to adapt diving for me. Although I am unable to dive anymore, you gave me an outlet when I needed one most and because of you I was able to start writing again. I felt free and I'm so thankful for that.

Alysha Glandon, for seeing me through all of high school and always providing me with their own poetry work to stimulate my mind and allow me to learn the ways of poetry.

Barbara Kowalinski - the Hero behind the

scrubs in the kindergarten room. You never had any requirement to be a friend to me, but you were anyway, you kept me alive through the final years of my sexual abuse. You made me feel safe enough with someone to finally disclose to my therapist. You changed my life for the better and I will forever be thankful to you. You are the kindest soul I have ever met; you gave me a safe place when I felt like nowhere was safe.

Madame Woolfries (Gill) - You only taught me one subject, French. But you knew me the best out of all of my teachers, you spent many recesses teaching me how to pronounce certain words so that I could sing in my mom's choir. You gave me a safe place to go to when I needed someone. You were the first teacher I ever trusted. Thank you for being so kind, giving, and pushing me to do my best. Merci Madame.

My New Path Family: Daneen Ens, Debbie Shea, Amy Alexander, Lee Anne Addley, and of course Yolanda Pascal. Every single one of these 5 amazing women, plus my two mystery staff members Cass and Barb have built a part of my personality, built my courage to go on stage and speak my truth, built my spirit and change who I am forever. These women have seen me through my worst, yet always shown me kindness. I will forever want to share my future with you because you made my past something I'm not afraid to look back on. Thank you for saving 16-year-old me and continuing to be a light in the darkest times of my life.

Finally, to Ms. Cahley Hackett, my grade 10 careers.

I shared my truth with you. I will forever

thank you. Always remember, you saved 15-year-old me. I wouldn't be alive to write this book without you.

Lastly, I would like to recognize all the teachers that I have had over the years. Each of you has created a different piece of who I am now. You will read some harsh stuff in here, stuff you may not have known. I give you permission to reach out if you have any questions or to just talk about how what I wrote made you feel. And please don't forget that you all have positive qualities as well.

PREFACE

The motivation to write this book came from realizing that writing to Carson meant healing. Carson has been through sexual abuse, suicidal ideation, hospital stay after hospital stay, in-patient for a year and a half, fear of being themselves, sexuality and gender.

Through every poem they wrote, they felt themselves healing a little bit more.

This book originally started as a writing challenge, but has become so much more.

Carson hopes that people struggling can relate to this book, and find some kind of comfort in their words.

1. TO THE KIDS IN MY ELEMENTARY SCHOOL

Remember those days, when I was that kid who you got placed with because you bullied everyone and no one stood up to you but me?

Remember those days that you thought it was funny to call me fat? Or the days that you told me I was too skinny?

Remember those days that you told me no one would ever be my friend?

Dear kindergarten teacher,
Why did you force me to be with those kids? Just because I can handle them doesn't mean it's safe for me, nor does it mean that I should have to deal with them.

Dear grade 1 EA,
Do you remember that day that those kid's, Ben's, Pokémon cards went

missing?
You made all of us tear apart our bags and the person I called my best friend took them out of her bag and put them right between my bag and hers so that no one could tell who had them?

Remember when I told you it wasn't me? Remember when I told you that same girl stole my little mermaid wallet that had money in it and you didn't believe me?
I found out she had it two years later when I saw her tossing it into the air at recess in grade 3.

Dear grade 2 teacher,
Why didn't you believe me when I told you the kids in my class were making me sad? This was the year I broke my foot, and my wrist. You didn't notice something was wrong, I understand.

Dear grade 3 teacher,
Didn't you wonder why I insisted on staying inside for recess? This year I

broke 4 bones in one year. Still, no one noticed. Kids have started to make fun of me. Making jokes about how I always hurt myself saying I'm faking and I'm doing it on purpose.

Dear grade 5 teacher,
Why didn't you ask me if I was okay when I came into school with bruises on my body and tears in my eyes?
When I hit someone why didn't you ask me if they were being mean?
When I was crying in the hallway, why didn't you notice?
By this time, I have had a total of 7 broken bones and still no one has asked, no one has noticed. Except for the kids now bullying me every day which you don't seem to notice.

Dear grade 6 teacher,
When I started failing your class, why didn't you ask why, why didn't you notice that I was getting smaller, why didn't you notice that I wasn't eating?

Dear grade 7 teacher,

You were my teacher in grade 6, how did you not realize something was wrong?

I spent all of my time with the kindergarteners because they were the only people who didn't make me feel like shit about myself.

Why didn't you follow me when I ran out of the class, why didn't you see that I hated my life?

How could you ignore the bruises and the silent screams, how could you not see that I was dying inside?

You have now seen me through 12 broken bones. Why didn't you clue in? Why didn't you ask?

Now you have started to laugh along with the kids saying I'm just breakable and I'm clumsy yet you still haven't asked me what happened. You didn't even ask me why I didn't want to participate in gym.

If you had asked, I would've told you my vagina was bleeding and torn apart and it hurt to walk, and not because I had my period.

Dear grade 8 teacher,

I don't understand. You saw three broken bones yourself in this year alone and a torn shoulder and you knew of the other 12 broken bones.
You saw days where I would spend hours in the bathroom alone and I would come back with a tear-stained face.
You knew I sat alone at recess in the corner reading books or recess with the primary kids and the kid in the wheelchair because him and his nurse were two of my only friends.

Why didn't you notice when I started wearing long sleeves in June, why didn't you notice when I started to refuse to wear shorts in gym class?
Where were you when I was sitting in the girl's bathroom for two hours with blood dripping down my arm because I hadn't had time to clean it off before I came to school?
I know you knew something was wrong because you never got me in trouble for not being in class and you always let my best friend Emily come to me in the bathroom even though she wasn't in

your class. So why didn't you say anything?

Dear Elementary school kids,
Do you remember the days when you called me a liar for saying things like "someone is taking pictures of you without your clothes on"?
I told you that because I was dissociating, that was part of what I was experiencing from my uncle.
So that was me trying to tell someone, me trying to figure out if that was right because that's what I had learned.
I had learned that adults have control that they can take pictures of whatever they want.
Everyone used to bully me because they thought I lied. I didn't lie, nothing I ever said was a lie, they were all things I had learned from my uncle, all things that had happened to me or that I had experienced.
And a year ago I thought I was crazy.
I thought I was so fucked up that no one could help me but I found the right people and I know that when I said

those things to people, I wasn't wrong, that was my way of asking for help.
Because though my conscious mind didn't know anything because I was drugged, my subconscious mind wanted me to ask for help.

So elementary school kids,
It turns out you were wrong. I am not who you said I was.
You will never understand what I went through but I will always remember what you said to me in my worst times.
None of you bothered to listen to what I was saying. You just made your assumptions
You will never know the real me and I feel sorry for you because you didn't choose to look past what I was saying and really hear me,
and now you will never know the great things about me.

2. TO MY FIRST LOVE

I would be lying if I said: "I'm fine"
I think of you at least a hundred times
'Cause in the echo of my voice I hear
your words
Just like you're there.
I can't hide from the truth that my heart
once loved you.
My heart breaks when I have the
thought that this is only in our past.
The goal of one day marrying you.

The goal of no matter who I meet in the
middle, we will always come back to one
another.

It's not easy. When you're not with me. I
remember you in everyday life.
I remember the support, throughout my

entire eating disorder from bulimia to anorexia to binge eating disorder, you were there all the way.

Allowing me to cry and recover, to throw up and recover, to eat and recover.

You made it possible for me to recover.

You made it so my life wasn't full of calorie counting.

You made it so I had a place to go away from my parents so I didn't want to die every day.

You taught me to be free, and to be strong willed and fight for what I want.

But I guess we had an expiration date.

So, I won't say I love you. It's too late.

All I will say is you will never leave my mind.

I may have chosen to leave, but that doesn't mean it hurt any less.

I never cried when we ended.

But I cry now.

I still cry to this day. Anyway, Goodbye, my love.I hope you find the one for you.

3. IN MY CAGE

Just hold on a moment, don't get any
closer
I just don't know if I can take it, it feels
like over exposure.
I've taken years to put up these walls,
why did I take them down for you;
are the thoughts that go through my
mind

Once again, I'm crumbled pieces on the
floor, irreparable.
I'm stumbling through my words as I
don't know how to feel, I want to die, I
want to cry, won't you ruin me again?
I dropped my walls for you, I let you in, I
thought it was destiny. But once again
I'm crumbled pieces on the floor.

You'll find me in my cage in the background of my life, you'll find me huddled in a corner once again shattered in a hurricane.

You'll find me in my cage, disappearing into the darkness.

You'll find me ruined once again.

Thank you for the memories. I'll hold them close to my heart.

4. TO THE PERSON WHO CHANGED ME THE MOST

You are a piece of charcoal.

You started as a person meant to keep me safe, care about me while I was in your care. You took me under your wing and forced me to become well.

You forced me to grow and experience new things. You showed me marijuana, you introduced me to the world of sex work, you believed in me when no one else did.
You came to the hospital when I tried to kill myself
and came home with me my first day home to make sure I was okay.
You then left me because I was:

"Too much, we were too much alike, we
were feeding off each other."
I then called you out on it and you
apologized and came back into my life.

After treatment,
You chose to take me in when I could no
longer live at home.
You would think at this point you would
start seeing me as an adult who was
now just living with you while working a
9-5 job.

But to you I was still below you. I wasn't
your equal. I was never equal to you. I
was always worth less.
I was always a small hamster that you
felt you had to carry and protect when
really,
I've become a wolf and you didn't even
see the change.

You don't know who I am, what I value
most,
who I value most,
you used to be someone I valued.

But I guess I was never something you
valued.

I'm sorry I was mistaken.
Now you are just the darkest coal I've
ever seen. Something I wish had never
entered my life.
Someone I wish had just given up
sooner and not hurt me like this.
I get it, you didn't know then. But still.
Fuck you.
 Fuck you for faking a role in my life, a
role you thought was huge
and yet still I let it go on
So I would be even more broken when
you left.

Just fuck you for coming back. And fuck
you for leaving again.

Goodbye Charcoal.

5. THE APOLOGY LETTER I DESERVE BUT NEVER RECEIVED.

Dear Carson Ellis,

I'm sorry I didn't feel I was strong
enough to look back on all we had and
apologize for some things

I want to get this thing off my chest
I've got no anger, got no malice
Just a little bit of regret

No, nobody else will tell you
So, there's some things I got to say
Gonna jot it down and then get it out
And then I'll be on my way
So here it is now,

1. I'm sorry that I chose to go to a
concert instead of holding you on the
one holiday you said you would always
need me
because every other year you had

admitted yourself to the hospital or tried to kill yourself
because otherwise you would get raped. I'm sorry I didn't take you seriously and been there for you like I should have.

2. I'm sorry that when you asked me to take the day off work because we were close to the end of our relationship and you wanted to work it out, I didn't.
I'm sorry I said I was going to work and went to Wasaga Beach — the one place you said you had always wanted to go — with our two roommates, without you when you thought I was at work.

3. I'm sorry you had to find out that we went to Wasaga Beach from someone else because he was home with a concussion.

4. I'm sorry I would say "hey babe, I mean Katie"

5. I'm sorry that when you gave me that letter, I didn't stop and talk about it with

you. Instead, I went to our roommates and they made you believe I was leaving you for good.

6. I'm sorry that the night you gave me the letter I didn't hold you while you vomited even though you cried and begged for me.

7. I'm sorry I wouldn't come to the hospital with you to get admitted when you wanted to kill yourself.

8. I'm sorry that I would never come after you when you were upset and try to help.

9. I'm sorry that I loved video games more than I loved you.

10. I'm sorry I let people influence me into someone that I am really not.

11. I'm sorry that I gave up on you when I said I never would.
12. I'm sorry that I said we would always be friends no matter what. I lied.

13. I'm sorry that when you finally got to do the nude photo shoot that I convinced you to do, I refused to go with you, leaving you alone to do something you were really excited for.

14. I'm sorry that I always said "once you have your service dog you won't need me anymore"

15. I'm sorry that I refused to help you shower leaving you dirty for days, unable to clean yourself until you eventually got a psw. And once you had a psw, I said I had no part of it. I left you to fight alone.

16. I'm sorry that I couldn't communicate that I was struggling with how much you were leaning on me so we could work it out.

17. I'm sorry that I didn't see that we needed to adapt our relationship, with me working and you unable to make food. We never talked about it, never

adapted.
18. I'm sorry that I broke the box of rainy-day money because I was mad and wanted to hurt you.

19. I'm sorry I made the choice between ruining a picture of us, or break the box, I shouldn't haven't done it, I shouldn't have even thought of hurting you like that.

20. I'm sorry that I made you wait 3 weeks before I decided if I wanted you.

21. I'm sorry that I told you we were over the day you were supposed to leave for Ottawa to work.

22. I'm sorry that I put so much pressure on you to look after me when you were only 16. And I'm sorry I never asked you about your mental health or who you are.

23. I'm sorry I wouldn't let you wear make-up or glasses without screaming at you because you didn't look like the

you I used to know.
24. I'm sorry I failed you, when you
needed me most.

25. I'm sorry that sometimes I would
look at you in the middle of sex and say
I see my dad.

26. I'm also sorry that when you broke
up with me, I said you're more fucked up
than my dad. And hurt me more than he
ever did.
The one who abused, raped, and used
every single kink thing on me. Burned
my hands to the point I feel nothing
when fire touches them. But no, I said
you were worse than that. That was
cruel, I am really sorry I broke you.

27. I am sorry that I called you "
transphobic". When the first time I told
you I was transgender, you tried to help
me pick out a male name, we tried the
name Ashton, but I wasn't ready for a
name.
And I'm sorry you don't know when that
changed.

We talked a lot about transitioning and I
always said I didn't want to take
hormones, I said I didn't know if I
wanted to keep certain body parts, so
you helped me learn to love every part
of me.

28. You always asked if I wanted you to
call me Ash and use male pronouns, but
I always said that I was a female to you,
and to use my birth name. I shared with
you my growth and what I wanted and
I'm sorry.

Oh, I feel so sorry I feel so sad.
You tried to help me, it just made me
mad,
And you had no warning, about who I
am,
I am sorry for what I've done.

Love, Ash"

Rainy
day
money

6. 78

I never thought you could change.
You're 78, you're stuck in many of your
ways, but one day you changed.

It all started with a girl named Emily,
seventh grade.
My first ever crush on someone that I
couldn't shake or ignore.
She was the most eye appealing person
I had ever met.
Her expression hard but her smile soft,
her hair gelled just right, her body slim,
her kindness shining through the hard
shell she put on.

I saw her and my heart stopped. But I
couldn't tell you because she was a girl
and not a boy like you had always
wanted.

78 years of the same ways.

This girl, Emily. She was my age; her
best friend was my best friend but we

didn't really know each other.

We spent a year together but never
talked and then everyone graduated.

We were left to fend for ourselves. Just
the two of us. I didn't know her, and she
didn't know me. We were like summer
and winter, like oil and water, so close
but never intertwining, and never
connecting.

Then one day, we did.

It just clicked. She was my best friend
and I was hers. My feelings for her grew
over the next two years and eventually. I
couldn't keep it in anymore.

I came home crying one day and you
looked at me and asked if I was okay.

I said no dad, I think I'm gay.

What I heard next was what I expected.
You said "Well Hunny, it's just a phase,
you'll be okay."

But through two abusive boyfriends and
two more years, I realized you were
wrong. I liked girls and I knew it for sure.

So, I tried coming out to you again.
This time was pretty much the same
reaction.
But after long talks and arguments and
lots of strong words from both of us.
You came up with this conclusion.

It was okay to be gay.

I remember the day like it was yesterday
though it was years ago,
You were walking me to the place where
I live, when you stopped me on the path
and said:
"Listen, I love you and you know that,
and if you want to marry a girl, I'm okay
with that."

I started crying and I looked at you and
asked" does that mean you will come to
my wedding?"
And you said "Of course."

78 years of the same things, the same
strong thoughts; then you changed.

You changed for me."

(January 2016)

7. TRIGGER WARNING ⚠:

SELF HARM

I've never felt more at home than with scars on my wrists.

I've never felt the warmth that self-harm brings from anything else.

I remember the first time like it was yesterday, the feeling of comfort, the feeling of safety and control, the feeling of home.

The pain I can control that no one can take away, the fear I felt in everyday life was melted away with each slice.

A part of me wishes that I never started, then maybe I wouldn't know what home felt like, or I'd have found home in something else.
But someday, I wish my home will change.

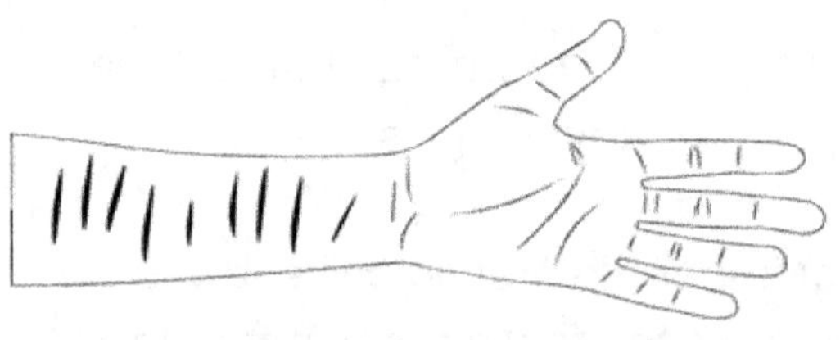

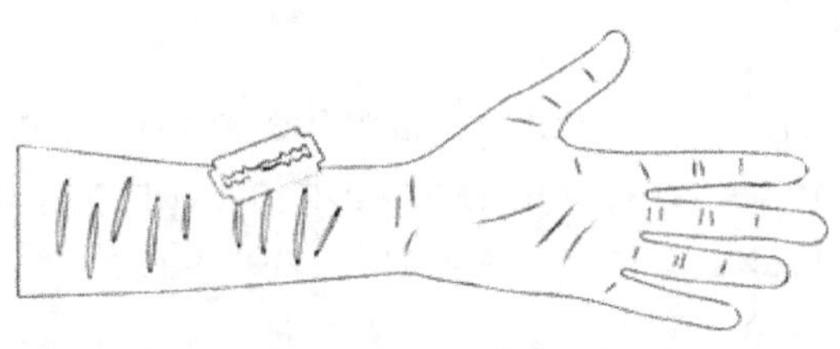

8. FEAR OF THE UNKNOWN

I believe in hopes, I believe in dreams, I
believe in change and I believe in
miracles
But I don't believe that I will ever be truly
happy.

Your shadow still haunts me every
moment of every day.

I am scared of looking over my shoulder,
because I feel like you will be there,
staring back at me with your smug smile
and sharp eyes like daggers.
Because of you, there are very few
places I feel safe.

You ruined the sweet child I once was.
You ruined my innocence.

You make me want to disappear.

You make me feel like everything is my fault.

You make me scream.

You make me cry.

When I finally feel happy, that's when you appear.

There is a part of me that wants to forgive you because you are so damaged that you took out all of your sadness and anger on a child; and for the longest time I did give you that grace because

I thought it was my fault, but it's not.

I was 3 when you started; I barely knew my colours let alone what abuse was. Maybe at some point you were kind, but that point is long gone.

You're grown up, and alcohol and drugs
have consumed your life.
You may have had stuff happen to you
that people don't know about but that
doesn't mean you couldn't have asked
for help and turned your life around.
You are the reason that I am afraid of
people, you are the reason I'm afraid to
get close.

I try not to let what you said and did
affect me, but somehow it always does.
I fear what others will do.
I fear what they will say, when they know
what you've done.

Will they blame me? Will they blame
you?
Will they hate me and leave?
Or will they stay and be there to catch
me when I fall to pieces?

Will they be there when the heart

monitor beeps and flatlines?

Will they cry once I'm dead?

Or will they say

"I knew she couldn't make it."

9. HERE I AM

Here I am in the school, struggling to
pay attention. Nobody hears me when I
speak.
Why do I speak at all?
There is only one who hears me, but
when she is away, I fall apart.
I shouldn't depend on her like that. But
there is nothing I can do to stop it. She's
been there for me all along
Not always on the front, but always
there in the background to catch me
when I fall.
When others fail, she's always there.

Here I am in the waiting room, I see the
doctor coming.
I don't know what to do.
I close my eyes and hope for him to go

away. I hope he's not here for me.

He stops to talk to the nurses, and so
my heart beat does too, but a few
minutes go by and then I hear what I
had dreaded

I hear my name come from between his
pursed lips.

I stand up and walk slowly towards him,
Fearing every step.
He smiles at me so I smile back.

We walk into a tiny room with a small
love seat and a wooden chair.

The walls are white with little nicks in
them from when fists have collided with
the wood, where chairs have scraped
over and over.

We talk and it's the hardest thing I've
ever done, but I do it because I know
that this is the only way I will get the
help I need.

He later tells me that I am a delight to
talk to. I wonder if that is really true?
That's for sure not what I heard from the
kids at school.

Here I am in this tiny room, the bed in
the middle, clothes on the floor,
The only thing that keeps me going is
the thought of you.

The bed is messy, things scattered all
around.
I look up at the ceiling and all I see is
white, no blue sky, no sun, no you.

I look out the window and all I see is the
roof, tall buildings that are way bigger
than me.
All those people who are free. I feel so
small and useless.
But yet I'm more than that.
I try to smile and think of you.

Here I am in this open space, people all
around me, smiling once again.
I hear your laughter and there is a
warmth in my heart.
I can't wait to feel you in my arms again,
my best friend.

Here I am, now, in my house,
Listening to the radio and singing along
without a care in the world.
Then I hear my parents fighting,
My heart breaks, and I feel like I'm
crashing.

But I remember that you said everything would be okay because I have you.

And that's all I need."
(Dedicated to My high-school best friend, Alysha Glandon, Oct. 2015)

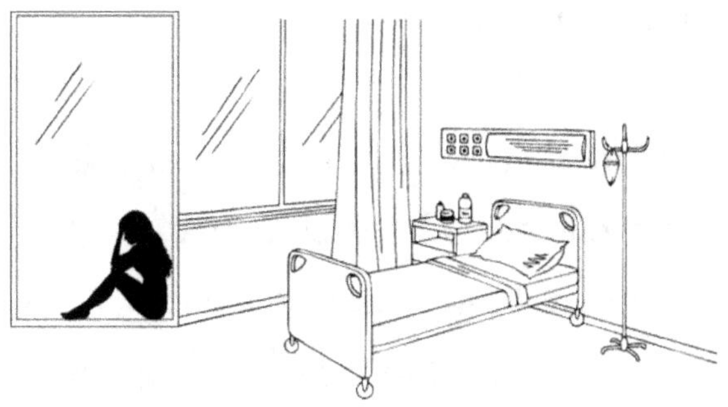

10. DISCONNECT

Sometimes I miss you when you're
standing right beside me,
We disconnect, it's like the phone lines
have fallen and intertwined in a different
way and I can no longer understand the
pulse of the electricity.

The phone cord falls to the ground, it's
like the line has been shredded and
somehow, I have to piece it back
together to be able to hear you again.

I am no longer like a bird, I cannot follow
your direction by the pulse running
through my feet,
I cannot see the sandwich that you grip
so tightly in your hand, as you run away
from the seagulls.

I cannot hear the slight noise you make
when you're happy,
I cannot smell your cologne. I cannot
speak your name.
I have gone senseless
I have gone blind, and deaf, mute, and
lost my sense of smell, and the feeling
in my limbs.

I am just stone, something you can talk
to that won't respond,
I am just a thing you can't hurt; I am just
a piece of granite.

Or maybe I'm a piece of lead that you
can write your stories down with.
Maybe I'm not as insignificant as I seem.
Maybe I'm used to writing stories of how
others feel, the stories of people's lives.

Maybe I am more than what meets the
eye
To you I look like a piece of greyish
black solid,

But to my owner, I am a pencil, that can
write a love song, write a novel, write a
poem.
I am not just nothing. I am me and that's
all I can be."

(July 2017)

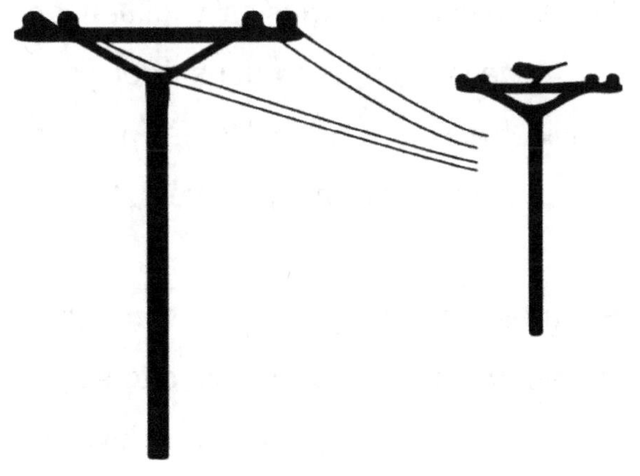

11. INDIFFERENT YET STILL BROKEN

You broke my heart; you broke my soul
you broke my spirit.

I've always been a musically influenced
girl. Always felt my emotions through
music, the lyrics and melodies spoke to
my soul and they had a conversation.

Pictures like a slide show run through
my head to the songs we used to sing
as anthems of our freedom and love.

Now a days when I hear music I feel
nauseous and my stomach sinks. My
heart filled with sorrow, so heavy and
suffocating.
I forget to breathe and when I do, I

struggle to inhale the air getting caught in my lungs, get nauseous and have to fight the urge to vomit. I haven't felt this feeling this bad since the year we met. As our relationship blossomed and our bond grew, my anxiety reaction went away for the most part
But the day you stopped talking to me that feeling I had before we met came back in full force.

Knocking me to the ground and isolating me for days
Not eating, just lying-in bed, forgetting to take my medication, forgetting to sleep. Most of the time I felt numb but then you would say something like "hi babe" and then immediately correct yourself "Sorry, I mean, hi Katie" and every time you did that my heart broke more, and I felt that overwhelming sadness and nausea.

I don't know.

Most days I feel indifferent, but

sometimes I have this feeling of a heavy

aura around me

that follows me everywhere and I just

cry that the whole day

Every time someone says something, it

could be anything, the heaviness is guilt

and sadness

Some days I feel as though the longer I

go without talking to him or really like

having his supporting me like he used to

I feel like I CAN live without her.

So now it's just learning how to live my

life again, alone.

But the problem is I'm scared.

I'm scared that I will forget how to act

around him.

I forgot how to act around my best friend

from 10 years old until 14.

I see her and I get the same anxiety I

get meeting new people

I'm scared but I will learn to fight this life

alone. Without you.

12. SUICIDE

Tigger warning ⚠

Why do you try and hurt me?
Why do you push me down and beat
me? Treat me like I'm nothing.
What have I don't to make you do this to
me? I cry each night wondering what I
did wrong.
I used to see you smile, but now...you
just frown.
That light that was in your eyes is gone
now, it's just darkness.
Why do you have to be so mean? What
did I do?
You used to try your best and now you
don't care.
I have to act like everything is okay
when I go to school.

Why do you have to make me hurt so
bad?

Why do you want me to cut my skin?
No one should have to go through that,
but I have to because of you.
Today, again you hurt me, just like
yesterday.

Why? Why do you choose to hurt me?
Especially this way?
It's cruel, it's mean.
Why the fuck do you do this? Why do
you do this to me?

I cut my skin once again because of
you. I cut as bad as I could until I was so
numb I could hardly feel it.
Now I'm awake debating suicide.

I can't take this anymore, you're killing
me.
I just want to die.
Why can't this be the end?

You asked me what I was doing in the
bathroom? I said peeing in peace.
But what I was really doing? Cutting my
skin piece by piece.

First thighs, then wrists, then arms, then
ribcage.

You made me this way. You made me
this monster.

I don't know why everyone hates me so
much, or maybe I do, because now I
hate me too.

(May 2015)

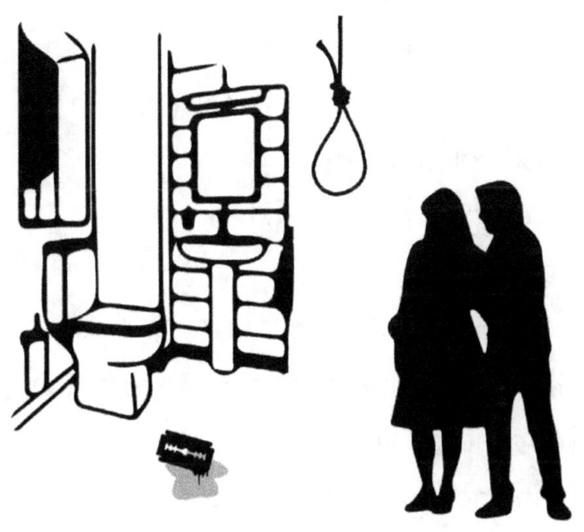

13. UNWANTED

I feel unwanted, like a useless plastic
bag floating in the wind.

I feel invisible like an unwanted painting
on a white slit canvas that's been torn
and damaged by years of lying on a
rose-coloured wall;
Drenched in water and chewed by
toddlers.

I've felt and breathed my own rejection,
A reflection I once knew,
I see no more. Wings once there,
Now clipped and rugged.
The me I once knew...where is she
now?

I bite my tongue and fear what I see,
Perhaps a beast, but inside of me?

I'm left here with the little faith I have,
shaking, wishing to fly, but never able to
soar.

Never to believe in myself.
I feel misplaced like I could be erased
from this place at any moment and it
wouldn't make a difference.

Once more, I become a toy on the top
shelf of the store.
Seen, yet unwanted.
C.E

4

14. MY FARWELL TO SELF HARM

Dear Self Harm,

I remember the blood.

Dripping from each cut slowly turning to beads on my skin and then flowing down my wrist into the sink leaving blood spots all over the sink and counter.

I remember the feeling of the blade being drawn across my own skin. The sting that comes first, followed by the rush of calm.

I'm not writing this as an instruction manual. But to say good bye to that little blade. It was my best friend and my worst enemy.

Dear self-harm, I don't hate you.

You made me feel when I didn't think I
could ever feel again.
But self-harm, on my good days I look at
my scars and I'm ashamed. I'm
ashamed I let you win.

Self-harm was the monster that followed
my every move whether it be a new job,
school, living somewhere else, losing
someone, it was around every corner

Always on the edge of rearing its ugly
head once again.

Dear self-harm, you were the first thing I
thought of when something made me
sad.

You were the first thing I thought of in
the morning.

The metal, the pain, the calm.

But I've trained my body to forget this
feeling over the last few years.
Sometimes relapsing and once again
remembering that feeling for a while,
stuck in a vicious cycle
I cannot think straight. All I can think is.
Sharpener. Blade. Cut. Relief.

Forgetting the steps that come after
regret, hurt of others, pain, pain, pain for
days, and scars. The scars that last a
lifetime to remind you each time you
look down at them that you lost a fight.

You lost a fight against yourself.
Self-harm won.

But when you've recovered, start
looking at your scars as warrior
symbols. Signs that you survived, that
you're alive and that you felt so deeply
in that moment it left permanent scars
on your skin.

And to me.
That is beautiful.

If you are weak. If you feel everyone's
life is better off if you're not in it
anymore. Stop. Breathe. Even if you
have to do it slowly. Choose life. You
can do this.
Because from what I've learned
You are more than this.

And it gets better. As hard as it is to
believe right now. Stop. Take a break.
Figure out what you love. And make it

your life.

So Self Harm: this is goodbye.

This is a message to thank you for being there when no one else was, but I have people now. I have my service dog Mystique, and I have my cat Peaches with me all the time. I have friends I can count on, and finally family as well.

Self-harm: Thank you. For your support through hard times and your unwavering presence.
But this is goodbye. Today I turn 19. I enter my adult years, and as I do I hope with everything I have, and work with everything I've got to leave you in my youth.
I hope to never see your ghost again. I hope you disappear from my life, never

to return.

Dear self-harm, Goodbye. And thank you.”

(C.E)

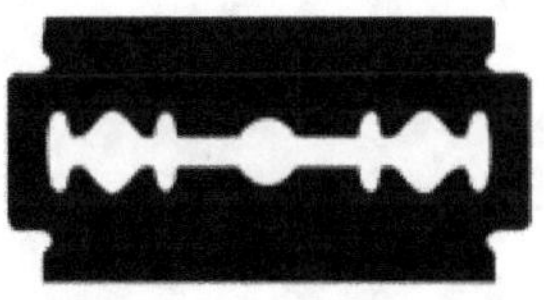

It was my best friend and my worst enemy

15. LITTLE RED CAPE

Sometimes it feels like the days are
merging together,
I can't tell the different between one day
and the next.
I can never really remember what has
happened. I just go through the motions.

Get up.
Shower.
Go to school.
Come home.
Sleep.
Repeat.

Same thing every day.
There are days where I can't see past
the cloud in my brain no matter how
hard I try.

There is a part of me that wants for it to
be possible to be given a miracle to feel
better,
But all of me knows that it will take a
long time. The good times last longer
now.
I cherish every moment.
But some days my heart feels so heavy
it doesn't feel like it's wearing its red
superhero cape anymore.
The depression has taken the red cape
and torn it to shreds,
The anxiety has told me that I can never
put it back together.
But my heart and a little whisper has
reminded me that everything can be
fixed with a needle, some thread,
and a little bit of love."

July 2017 (C.E)

16. WHITE GIRL

To the person who calls me white girl
My ancestors weren't taken hostage in
the holocaust and they weren't
imprisoned by a person forcing them to
be slaves. So, to you I'm just another
person with white privilege.

But I can tell you that yes, that is still
true in society, but that doesn't mean
that my life is any easier than yours, it's
just different.

You just see me as a white person with
white privilege not someone who has
been beaten down by the government,
been slammed against lockers in high
school hallways, been beaten until
bloody then raped.

I see that white privilege is a very real thing. I do my best to not use it, but I can't stop being white. I can't change the past and make bad things happen to my family, I can't go back and stop bad things from happening to yours.

All I can do is fight for both of our freedoms and fight for injustices and hope that not everyone has the same feelings towards me as you do.

Yes, I'm white but that doesn't mean I'm more or any less than you and that doesn't give you the right to make fun of the fact that I'm white.

Because in my genes, my chromosomes tell me that I'm white no matter what I do. As you can't change the fact that you're brown.

I am a person of culture. Many different cultures that I am proud to be a part of.

I'm like a polar bear.

White but black underneath

I'm not a person of colour, black or white or anything in between I am just a human.

Who wants to change the world. And I could do that being any colour. It's not the colour the person is, it's who the person chooses to be.

I hope that you change your mind, because after all, I'm dating your daughter."

2017 (C.E)

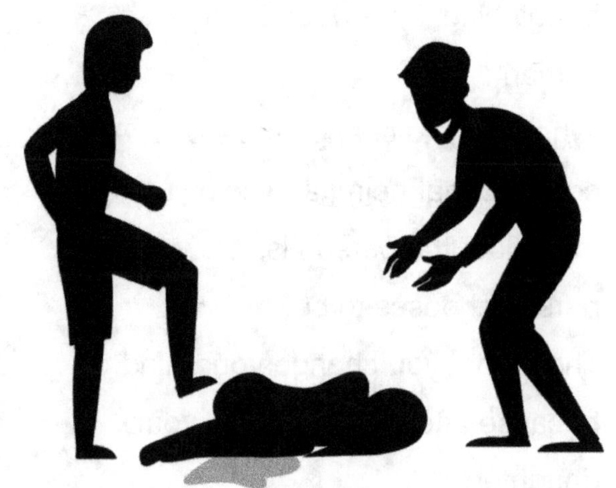

17. TO THOSE OF YOU AFFECTED BY DEMI LOVATO'S OVERDOSE.

I'm here. I get it. It's heart breaking not just because she almost died, but because she was my role model, she was clean 6 years. She gave me hope, she was proof that recovery was possible.

But now she's proof that no matter how hard I try I will always fall back.

My heart says "you gave up, you stopped fighting," but my mind says "she was trying, she has a mental illness, her mind was saying she needed drugs to feel okay, to survive."
I am angry because she was the whole

reason I got into recovery, she talked to
me in my darkest hour and told me to
hold on, so I did, but she gave into her
illness.

I know it's hard, I have compassion and
I know mental Illness very well because
I deal with it myself everyday, so it's
hard for me to be angry. But I am.

I try my best to forgive her but it's hard
right now.
But no matter what, she will always be
my hero all the way through her mental
illness
And I know one day I will stop hurting, it
may just take a while.

(C.E)

18. PIPE POEM

There goes another one,

One foot down the pipe.

Sliding farther and farther down the cold
metal sides to a darkness I have yet to
know.

If I could, I'd unfuck you. Take away all
the orgasms, take away all that we had.

Take away the hickies and the making
out.

Maybe then I would forget the feeling of
your lips pressed against mine, the
sweet smell of your breath as your
tongue reached mine.
Maybe then I could forget you.

C.E

19. SENSES

We all know a human being has 5
senses,
Sight, smell, taste, touch and hearing.

But what happens when you lose one or
more of those senses?

I grew up with a mom that was
passionate in everything she went after,
a mom that spent days in hospitals with
me, a mom who taught academic
English in high school for 30 years, but
why is my mom different?

My mom just happens to be blind.
When I was 3 and I made a picture, I
knew that I had to explain what it looked
like, and I knew that I had to let my mom
touch it.

My mom sees through touch, my mom
sees through hearing, and my mom
sees through taste.

The face they make when they eat

something new, makes my heart light up.

But you know one thing? My mom never learned to eat corn. My mom will take random bites off of the cob and still end up not missing anything.

My mom taught me about bras, she did this by feeling me to make sure it fit because she couldn't see it and I didn't know how it should fit.

My mom taught me that when you are expecting orange juice and you taste milk you immediately want to vomit.

My mom taught me that vagisil does not make good toothpaste.

My mom taught me that immediately smelling something that is handed to you to make sure it's clean is normal.

My mom taught me to smell things before I eat them because my dad is terrible at throwing things out.

My mom doesn't judge someone based
on their looks,

My mom doesn't judge someone on how
put together they look

My mom taught me that life is so much
more than what you see.

My mom taught me that I can use all of
my senses and get so much more
information than just from my eyes.

My mom taught me a source of
freedom.

MacBeth

20. THE TRUSTWORTHY MAN

To the man who taught me what real trust is.

This man came into my life by accident and has become a part of my world.

He has held my hand while I have sobbed, has listen to my rants, has heard all of my poems and still wants to hear more.

He's watched me throw up, he's watched me have panic attacks, slice my arm open and needing stitches, he's seen our mutual partner overdose.

This man makes me food when I can't.

This man will get up no matter how he is

feeling and get whatever I need if I can't do it.

This man will feed bugs when I'm not able to. He offers his help any chance he can.

His smile is like a field of fresh dandelions, so bright and beautiful you cannot take your eyes off of it.

His eyes have a mystery behind them, yet a spark inside them.

This man has proven me time and time again that I can trust him.

That he's safe.

That he's not going to hurt me, and he's not going to leave me.

This man has chosen to love me when I
am at my sickest and he knows that.

Only 2 days before had we started
dating when I found out I was really sick.
I immediately gave him an out but he
didn't take it.

Only a couple days after, he took me to
the dollar store
I saw a sunflower I couldn't kill and
really wanted but couldn't afford, so he
bought it for me.

A couple days later he came home with
a rose that I couldn't kill because I've
been saying I've wanted one.

He will never take the out. This is all
proof.

This is John.